Philip Connell

Poaching on Parnassus

A Collection of Original Poems

Philip Connell

Poaching on Parnassus
A Collection of Original Poems

ISBN/EAN: 9783337168018

Printed in Europe, USA, Canada, Australia, Japan

Cover: Foto ©Thomas Meinert / pixelio.de

More available books at **www.hansebooks.com**

POACHING

ON

PARNASSUS,

A COLLECTION OF ORIGINAL POEMS.

BY PHILIP CONNELL,

AUTHOR OF "ORWIN AND SEBANA," ETC.

"And thou, sweet Poetry, thou loveliest maid,
Still first to fly where sensual joys invade;
Dear lovely nymph, neglected and decry'd,
My shame in crowds, my solitary pride."—GOLDSMITH.

MANCHESTER: JOHN HEYWOOD, 143 DEANSGATE.
LONDON: SIMPKIN, MARSHALL, & CO.
1865.

DEDICATION

TO THE

Right Honourable Lord Farnham, K. P.

My Lord,

  Seeing that in a dedication the simple expressions of gratitude may appear like adulation, I shall merely observe that mine is an humble return of the bread cast on the waters many years ago, when your Lordship's princely gift of the works of the English poets tempted me to commit the sin of rhyming—and that the glimpses of rural happiness which may be found in the following poems were evoked by those which I have seen realized through the munificence of your Lordship and Lady Farnham in the happy cottage homes around the haunts of my childhood.

 I have the honour to write myself,

My Lord,

Your Lordship's most devoted servant,

PHILIP CONNELL.

PREFACE.

Perhaps I may be pardoned for observing here, by way of preface, that the writing of the following poems has been the occasional recreation in his leisure hours, " few and far between," of a self-taught peasant, the language of whose childhood was Irish, which he even yet finds the easiest-fitting dress for his feelings. Therefore the critic who will plume himself on discovering errors in this work may exult in breaking a fly on the wheel.

It may be asked, ' Thus unprepared, why venture before the public ?" To this I reply, that as " Fools will rush where angels fear to tread," this is not my first venture. The author of " The Medal and Glass," so much applauded by Father Matthew and the editor of " The Cottage Journal," dubbed in the public press as the " Rural Reformer," is yet well remembered in the vicinity of his old home of Auburn Cottage, among the vallies of Breffni.

Another reason for my coming forward now is, that Education being the great topic of the day, I fancied that many might wish to read a work written by one of the few surviving pupils of the old Irish Hedge-school, such as I have tried to describe in my poem of "The Gregory Day."

In one of these schools I spent six months, and picked up the remainder of my education on winter nights, attacking Euclid without a teacher, and got a glimpse of the *Ass's Bridge* by the light of a bogdeal fire.

Yet all this but convinces me the more of the salutary influence of a regular education; because a want of confidence in my own acquirements, together with a certain natural timidity (which doubtless the companionship of schoolfellows in childhood would have rubbed off), has always impeded my progress in life, and leads me to the conclusion that storing the young mind with desultory knowledge is more injurious than otherwise; that it is the training to habits of order, of submission, and of patient application (as carried out in good schools), engrafted on a proper knowledge of, and a proper reverence for the truths of Christianity, which produces a good and useful man, and lays the foundation of success in the bustle and turmoil of life.

THE MANCHESTER ALBERT MEMORIAL.

Inscribed to Thomas Fairbairn, Esq., Chairman of the Manchester Art Treasure Exhibition. Inaugurated by H.R.H. Prince Albert, May 5th, 1857.

To Thee whose care and classic taste,
   Devis'd for us that splendid vision,
Which shining still " O'er mem'ry's waste "
   We oft recall in dreams Elysian.

Th' Art Treasure, where the march of Mind
   Might pause rejoicing wearied never,
And feeling hearts and souls refin'd
   In Beauty own " A Joy for ever."

To Thee who like Aladin rais'd
   That wond'rous magic palace – where
Great Albert's self in wonder gaz'd,
   And lov'd alone to linger there.

To Thee I tune these artless lays,
   My grateful offering on that shrine,
Which loyal Manchester doth raise,
   Long to outlast this wreath of mine.

I.

'TWAS meet that Rome which could in pastime view
   The gladiator's agonizing pain ; (1)
Should raise commemorative columns to
   The bloodstain'd Cæsars great thro' millions slain.

II.

'Tis meet that Paris prodigal of blood,
    Too well accustom'd to the cannon's roar,
Should celebrate their names who only could
    Obtain renown thro' floods of reeking gore.

III.

'Tis meet that Manchester, whose quiet fame
    Arose with the majestic march of mind,
Should thus perpetuate *His* honour'd name,
    Whose life-long work was to improve mankind.

IV.

The holy joy of happy cottage homes,
    The peace of christian love to multiply;
To rescue science from neglected tomes,
    And send her forth the harbinger of joy.

V.

To blend the human race in social love,
    To win for Ceres Amalthea's horn ; (2)
The heart by Education to improve,
    And blessings plant for millions yet unborn.

THE MANCHESTER ALBERT MEMORIAL.

VI.

To congregate the nations of the earth,
    In friendly contests of artistic skill ;
To ope' the porch of fame to modest worth,
    Such the imperial task he would fulfil.

VII.

While the more selfish trod in quest of sway,
    The hackney'd paths of Politics or War,
He—far above—serenely led the way,
    Of peaceful Wisdom and outsoar'd them far.

VIII.

No higher glory could the Cæsars share,
    Than the procession in triumphal show,
With harness'd Princes scowling in despair,
    The mutilated wrecks of war and woe.

IX.

How poor ! compared to that auspicious day,
    When (thousands eager for the glad surprise)
'Twas *his* supreme enjoyment to display
    The rich " Art Treasure " to our wondering eyes.

X.

How grand, how radiant with pure happiness,
    Shone his imperial brow while all around,
Shar'd in his exquisite unselfish bliss,
    Silent, entranc'd in reverence profound.

XI.

When all at once like an Armidian scene,
    The glorious inspirations met their eyes :
Of Rapheal, Ruben, Angelo, Loraine,
    Murillo, Turner, Wilkie and Maclise.

XII.

These pure delights, as yet but little known,
    To share alike with all was his endeavour,
That even the humblest with himself might own,
    " A thing of beauty is a joy for ever."

XIII.

Alas ! that choicest fruit will earliest fall,
    That noblest souls are soonest call'd away,
That but a few revolving years were all,
    Of life accorded from that very day.

XIV.

That the pure taste he kindly would direct,
    Our cruder minds to foster and refine,
Should but mature our judgments to select,
    For his own Monument this rich design.

XV.

He whom the millions taught would more delight,
    Than all the transient glories of a crown,
And thus unsought obtain'd a name more bright,
    Than ever rose from carnage to renown.

XVI.

How dim is Hannibal's and Cæsar's fame?
    Cypress and yew among their laurels twin'd;
While gentle Plato's venerated name
    Serenely grand, is dear to all mankind.

XVII.

Thus when in future years some Hume or Scott,
    May celebrate Victoria's happy reign;
When Alma and Magenta are forgot,
    Shall *Albert's* name a household word remain.

XVIII.

Relentless Death ! didst thou rejoice to show,
   That neither wisdom, genius, birth, or power,
A sovereign's anguish, or a nation's woe,
   Could stay thy fatal stroke a single hour.

XIX.

Yet on the fast receding world's dim shore,
   Not all Thy terrors could that soul dismay,
While Faith and Hope triumphant led him o'er,
   Thy shadowy valley to eternal day.

XX.

Insatiate Death, how awful thy approach,
   Even to the just—what melancholy gloom
Surrounds thy presence,—how thy withering touch
   Spreads desolation in the happiest home.

XXI.

Cheerless, Balmoral are thy lonely shades,
   What awful silence lingers in thy halls ;
The huntsman's cheer from out thy echoing glades,
   No more resounds along the waterfalls.

XXII.

Forsaken Osborne, how thy floating leaves,
    Falling so sere and slow 'mid Summer smiles,
Thy wailing breezes, and low sobbing waves,
    Try to console the Daughter of the Isles.

XXV.

Nor Kew nor Buckingham delight her more,
    Capricious grief no haven can prefer ;
Of all her realms from Inde to Labrador,
    Frogmore alone seems all the world to her.

XXIV.

Farewell great prince and from thy place on high,
    (If souls departed deign to look below,)
Thou see'st a Queen in tears, a nation sigh,
    And thus their sorrows in memorials shew.

XXVII.

Thou wilt see thy offspring multiply on earth,
    Uniting Europe in domestic ties ;
And teaching nations the transcendant worth
    Of early culture from the good and wise.

XXVIII.

Thou wilt see thy adopted country rising still,
   In arms and arts, with peace and plenty crown'd;
Thy children's children's royal offspring fill
   The page of History, honour'd and renown'd.

XXIX.

And while as ages pass like summer's prime,
   Successive crops of men by Death are shorn;
All drifting down the mighty stream of time,
   To the unknown interminable bourne.

XXX.

When Bennett, Heywood, Potter, Mackie, Watts
   And Goadsby, in the past half-seen afar,
Sink in the mist of years (as Phoebus sets),
   With Cheetham, Byrom, Dee and De le Warre. (*t*)

XXXI.

After revolving years are pass'd away,
   When we shall all have moulder'd into dust;
When little children, stopping from their play,
   Shall ask their sires," Whose is that ancient bust?

XXXII.

Or why this antiquated pomp of stone,
  Now half defac'd by Time's destructive wings?
Shall greybeards answer—" Thus, in ages gone,
  Manchester crown'd the father of our kings."

XXXIII.

"Albert the Good," who as each school boy reads,
  The "Exhibition" to its triumph led;
Who first drew breath in Rosenau's sylvan shades,
  And last in Windsor, making nations sad.

XXXIV.

" But that was long ere the electric flame
  Had superseded gas—ere men could fly—
When clumsy railway engines went by steam,
  And Kings sent forth their thousands to destroy.

XXXV.

" When Palestine was held by Moslem foe,
  Ere yet Columbia own'd a monarch's nod;
When strangulations were a public show,
  And pews were rented in the house of God."

ON ALDERMAN GOADSBY'S GIFT

Of a Statue of the Prince Consort to the City of Manchester.

WHOEVER of Achiles reads,
    But thinks of Homer's fame;
Or fancies Richard's fearful deeds,
    Forgetting Shakespere's name.

St. Peter's yet to living men
    Great Angelo recalls;
And who but thinks of honour'd Wren,
    When gazing on St. Paul's.

So while that Cenotaph appears,
    Adorning Albert Square;
Shall Goadsby's name in other years,
    Be the historian's care.

LINES TO MR. ISAAC HOLDEN, Jun.,

On his Drawing of the Prestwich Lunatic Asylum.

WRAPT in deep wonder on thy work I gaze,
    That with such truth and elegance pourtrays
The splendid scene, which, when thy grave is old,
The wondering traveller will yet behold
O'er Prestwich woods, where soon in sad repose,
Shall broken hearts life's weary voyage close.
  While gazing on thy sketch, O, might I share
Such inspirations, and in fancy there,
Pry, like Asmodeus, into ward and cell,
And paint their phantasies who there shall dwell:
Noting of various minds, the various moods,
As each apart o'er his own frenzy broods.
  From yonder pillar'd corridor below,
A tall thin man comes forth demurely slow;
His hollow eyes scowl moody on the ground,
Or, if perchance, he raise them gazing round,
What pen can paint his eager aimless stare?

Like one who listening stands in mortal fear,
Restless and quick his glance, still muttering low,
Each gleam of sense but brings a glimpse of woe ;
Bills, speculations, bankruptcies, arrears,
Endorsements, mortgages and railway shares.

  Midst the incurables, within his cell,
The moon-struck lawyer I at once can tell;
With brief in hand he holds the court at bay,
Quotes Cooke and Blackstone, makes as clear as day
The point at issue, replications, deeds,
Replevins, judgments and rejoinder pleads ;
Then blythly capers round the dancing ring,
And now with Old King Cole sits down to sing.

  Lo, the craz'd Architect, once in whose brain
Did genius, order, taste and judgment reign ;
Till elevations, sections, tangents, signs,
Equations, segments, angles and designs,
Confus'd the conformation of his brain,
And on the ruin science beam'd in vain—
As broken mirrors strange reflections cast,
His shiver'd genius sparkles to the last;

And entering on his wonted path again,
A glimpse of reason flashes on his brain,
And he exclaims, " This building is well plan'd,
The sexes separate on either hand—
The various wards for various stages where
The idiot must not at the madman stare,
Nor moody Hypocondriac fret to see
How much more mad he yet thro' time may be.

The craz'd Accountant comes, I hear him rave,
And aimless talk with calculations weave ;
Twice four are eight and nine are seventeen ;
I heard a blackbird sing—God save the Queen,
And country too—eight into thirty-five
Goes four times—how can any nation thrive,
So deeply tax'd as this ?—and three remains;
The Yankees are keen fellows—whips and chains,
Straight waistcoats, and dark chambers, three times three
Make nine—yon keeper comes in quest of me.

With brow elate and features wildly grand,
Behold the hair-brain'd Actor proudly stand;
My name is Norval—wife ! I have no wife—

LINES TO MR. ISAAC HOLDEN.

An envious thrust from Tybalt hit the life—
Of poor Bob Acres at his finger ends —
But tell me Fusbus, first and best of friends,
Must Shylock really have his pound of flesh
Off Hamlet's ghost ? he should have din'd on fish—
It must be so. Plato thou reasonest well—
Bring with thee airs from Heaven or blasts from Hell.
Thou com'st in such a questionable shape—
Ha ! tis my keeper how shall I escape ?
Behind the chapel is my safest course—
A Horse, a horse, my kingdom for a horse.

   Beneath yon lonely chesnut tree apart,
With throbbing brow, flush'd cheek and pulseless heart,
The fragile ruins of a lovely maid
Recumbent rests beneath the sombre shade,
Smiling like glow-worm on a new made grave,
Her thin long fingers blades of spear-grass weave,
And singing sweetly, beautifully slow,
Some ballad old that tells of lover's woe,
Now sadly, sweetly, softly murmuring o'er,
Pathetic scraps from Byron, Keats or Moore,

And now relating to the viewless wind
Constantia's love by piety refin'd.
Poor Werter's grief, Ophelia's swanlike strains
And Jeanie weeping for poor Effie Deans,—
Then starting suddenly with keen wild eye
She looks afar—then with a broken sigh
She turns her thoughts within—what meets she there?
Fragments of broken hopes mid dark despair.

Perched in an attic window mounted high,
Pale and resign'd with wildly vacant eye
The wreck of genius sits—still can I trace
Deep musings in that intellectual face
One grand discovery he had sought for years
Which found at last, had recompens'd his cares
When lo a wealthy boor his fame purloin'd
And crush'd for ever his distracted mind
His fit returns, he gazes all around
And thus comes forth his coloquy profound—
" Yes on a lofty slip of table land
This building is appropriately plan'd
Extensive prospects on all sides appear,

Mountains afar, and woods and waters near,
Along the North and East the healthful gale
Sweeps o'er the ancient heights of Rosendale
And Southward at due distance the huge hive
Of busy Manchester is all alive,
Its towering chimnies, domes and steeples rise
In strange confusion thro' the hazy skies;
There Broughton glimmers in the evening sun;
Here Cheetham Hill o'ertops the vapours dun:
There Kersal Moor the same bleak front doth shew
That met the view Eight hundred years ago,
When Cluniac Monks there with their God did dwell
Within the precincts of its holy cell
Here close at hand thro' ancient wood and vale,
I mark the winding Irwell slowly steal
To seek repose from sluices dams and mills,
Compell'd since issuing from his native hills
To turn some thousand busy wheels and force
O'er cascades, banks, and wiers, its onward course.
Hard working river, whose exertions yield
More gold than Lydian Pactoles reveal'd—

LINES TO MR. ISAAC HOLDEN.

Here just at hand the cheerful village smiles
Amidst its pastures, hedges lanes and stiles
And sere and grey, beneath the weight of years
Lordly and lone, the ancient church appears
To contemplate as if with pensive pride
The fragile villas rising on each side
Again to perish like so many more
That rose—looked round, and vanished heretofore.
As these must also with Time's other spoils
When children's grandchildren will fill these Aisles.—

Thus well and wisely have the good designed
This calm Asylum, where the wounded mind
The scoffs of an unpitying world can shun,
And suffer (if it must) unseen, unknown—
Mid scenes domestic, peaceful, humble, plain,
The dreamy maniac feels at home again,
And hears once more the soothing sabbath bell—
The same sweet sounds his childhood loved so well,
And views the church and parsonage close by
Recalling former scenes of homefelt joy
And who can tell what peace of mind is there,

For wounded spirits met in mutual prayer,
For those o'er whom the good can only mourn,
Who had met elsewhere but mockery or scorn,—
For those who happly feel more real joys,
In their wild wanderings than the mighty wise—
Since Reason ever with our hopes at strife,
Views but the grim realities of life ;
Children are happy in their artless joy,
Ere comes the lamp of Reason to destroy,
And when in sleep that lamp no longer gleams,
How bright, how glorious is the land of dreams.
The Lunatic who deems himself a king,
Tastes all the happiness a crown could bring
Without its cares.—Then, who can ascertain.
Which are the most content the craz'd or sane ?

THE FIRE HORSE.

Written to Isaac Holden, Esq., Architect, on the Opening of the East Lancashire Railway, Sept. 25th, 1864.

I.

THE mighty Fire Horse panting foam'd,
    Impatient of delay ;
And clouds of smoke from his nostrils broke,
    As he bounded away, away !

II.

Old echoes hear and quake with fear,
    From cavern'd rock and hill,
And the trembling ground replied around,
    To his whistle wild and shrill.

III.

With the hurricane speed of the North wind free'd
    He shoots o'er the quaking plains,
For the giant might of England's wealth,
    Invigorates his veins.

IV.

From the strange wild sound o'er the fields around
    The herds in amazement fly ;
And the wondering sun his speed outdone,
    Stands still in the mid-day sky.

V.

Onward the Fire Horse wends his way,
    A comet with shining tail,
And he starts from their sleep of a thousand years,
    The echoes of Rosendale.

VI.

The old hills split his approach admit,
    And the tunnell'd rocks also,
In their bowels feel his iron heel,
    As he roars in the dark below.

VII.

On the ancient heights of Rosendale,
    The shades of the dead are seen ;
Arous'd from their sleep in the cold grave deep,
    They stand in warlike sheen.

VIII.

With kirtle scant, Old John of Gaunt,
 In helm and hauberk high;
And at his side in warlike pride,
 His bearded progeny.

IX.

The Edwards, Henries, Richards, each
 Half drew his shining blade,   [light
And they frown'd in their might by the strange blue
Which their own reflection made.

X.

" Saying " Who be those that " Our *Red Rose* "
 Dares on their shields display,
Have the Dogs of York been again at work
 While we were wrapt in clay? "

XI.

But a smile of grace illum'd each face
 As the warriors chanc'd to spy
These words beside their Rose of pride
 " The East Lancashire Company."

XII.

All right, cried John, my sons march on,
    Complete your wondrous plan;
In peace or war shall Lancaster's Star
    Shine in Britannia's van.

XIII.

Whilst onward wrought thro' hills remote
    Your Firehorse wends his way,
Shall trade resound and wealth abound
    Among these dingles grey.

XIV.

Till plenty bless these barren wilds,
    And happy homes prevail—
Where the wolf and boar were wont to roar—
    In the forests of Rosendale.

A WINTER NIGHT IN MANCHESTER.

WHEN surly Winter o'er the naked earth
    Sends forth the stormy terrors of the North;
When Irwell thundering from the Yorkshire hills
Victoria Bridge up to the keystone fills.
When fogs in Deansgate veil the dusky air,
And winking gaslights yield a sickly glare;
When names of streets no more on corners guide,
Bewilder'd housewifes wandering far and wide;
When colour'd lamps, with faintly lurid ray,
But dimly shew the blinking drunkard's way.
When mufflers, furs, and asthmas are the mode,
And dark umbrellas hide the miry road;
When mid a wilderness of chimneys high
The palid sun beneath a troubl'd sky—
Just peeps above the snow-cap'd roof at noon;
Then leaves the world to cold and darkness soon.
While sleet and snowdrifts usher in the night,
Then shivering Winter is establish'd quite:—

A WINTER NIGHT IN MANCHESTER.

At Evening bell when Warehouse, Office, Forge,
Workshop and Mill their thousand hands disgorge;
Where may these countless sons of toil repair
Meet recreation for the night to share?
If to the streets there rang'd on either hand
In tawdry shreds alluring harlots stand
With aching hearts and palid faces veil'd
In paint and smiles, alas, how ill-conceal'd!
If to the Beerhouse there a maudlin crew
Their ribald, rank, disgusting jests renew;
If to the Theatre—with Shakespeare's art,
Tho' Brook and Dillon try to touch the heart,
Their grandest strokes what feeling heart enjoys
While ruffian, ragged gods renew their noise?

   Far other scenes now bless the workman's night,
In slippers easy, chair, and shirtsleeves white,
With hair to one side comb'd, and well-wash'd face
Radiant with happiness—whilst in her place
The very cat enjoys her evening nap,
Purring her grateful anthems in his lap.
And ever as he casts around his eyes

A look meets his, beaming with hopes and joys,
And quiet happiness—his own dear Bess
Nursing their baby boy in fond caress,
His vermil' lips around the nipple press'd,
And half his cheek hid in her milkwhite breast :
There sits the workman in his happy home,
The fire fair blazing round the cheerful room,
The carpet brush'd, the grate and fender bright,
The polish'd table glancing to the light,
The hearth pure white, the chimneypiece array'd
With dogs and shepherds nestling in the shade;
The simple shelves with glass and china bright,
The busy bare-faced clock not always right;
The baywood bookcase, full, select, but small,
Curtain'd with crimson, pendant on the wall,
And hung around—the lovely, good, and wise
Look from their maple frames, with living eyes.
Midst maps unroll'd that to his eyes display
Leagues upon leagues of countries far away.
Nor these alone endear the workman's home,
Behold what friends to cheer his evenings come

From "The Free Library" lo! Johnson, Blair,
Rollins, Macaulay, Robertson appear,
Boyle, Newton, Bacon, Tillotson and Hume,
With all the classic minds of Greece and Rome;
While Bulwer, Ainsworth, Lever, Boz and Scott
Recite their Thousand tales in social chat.

Behold him next wrapt up in scenes sublime!
Scenes that from Poet's brain in olden time
Flash'd forth electric, and in verse enshrin'd
Still holds a magic influence over mind,
With Homer now he mounts the Trojan wall,
Now sails with Virgil where strange oceans roll;
Now Shakspeare's magic bids his bosom swell,
Now follows Milton thro' the gloom of hell;
With Job sublimely rapt, in wonder gaze,
Or join the son of Jesse in prayer and praise.

EPITHALAMIUM

MARCH 10th. 1863.

WHILE Wars their demon revels hold
    Throughout the New World and the Old,
Within fair Britain's favour'd Isles,
From sea to sea rejoicement smiles
In cottage, hall, and village green
To welcome England's future Queen.
Hark to the loud protracted cheers
Each echoing hill its neighbour hears!
Llewelyn from his summit hails
His own especial Prince of Wales,
Old Scafell answers thro' the night,
And dark Ben Nevis from whose height
Rebellowing echoes waft it o'er
To Carntoul on Erin's shore;
All sending forth one joyous peal—
"Hail, lovely Star of Denmark, hail!"
  Nor less from hyperborean skies
Come bursts of simultaneous joys.
Where shades of heroes boisterous all

Illuming each his airy hall
With Northern lights, forget at last
Their deadly feuds of ages past;
Lo, Guthrum grasping Alfred's hand,
Fierce Lodbrog break his dreadful brand,
Old Starno smiling greets Fingal,
And Sitric grieves for Brian's fall,
These bless the Regal Virgin mild,
Thro' whom they now are reconcil'd—
But say, O Royal Maiden fair
While welcomes meet thee everywhere.
Do retrospective dreams restore
Thy childhood's home near Elsinore?
Nay, Regal Virgin, rather smile—
Calm are the skies o'er Britain's Isle,
And English hearts tho' rather slow
In coming out, more warmly glow.
To Love and Friendship longer true—
Late comes the Oak leaves into view;
But when December sweeps the hill
Their parents' boughs they shelter still.

THE COTTER'S SUNDAY MORNING,

In humble imitation of Burns' "Cotter's Saturday Night."

I.

TIS Sunday morning, from serene repose (5)
    The Cotter starts at Five, accustom'd well
To watch that hour—but takes another doze,
    For on that morn there peals no startling bell,
    Those who like him must toil, alone can tell
The full satiety which he enjoys;
    Of sweet delicious rest he takes his fill;
As playing with his little ones he lies,
While each to win a smile some fond endearment tries.

II.

Not so his faithful wife, on her that morn
    Devolves the task their homestead's charge to view,
Startling the skylark from the aged thorn,
    Her winding ways appear in greener hue,
    Along the fields where slowly o'er the dew

She genily drives her liberated kine;
  Next in the kitchen yard what swarms pursue
Her busy steps—hens, turkies, geese and swine,
All for their morning meal in mingl'd murmurs whine.

III.

Meantime their kitchen is a busy scene,
  Where all the elder children now prepare
Their sunday dress, that tidy, neat and clean
    They in due time may reach the house of prayer,
    And all things have a comfortable air;
Sleek heads, clean faces, caps and polish'd shoes,
  The chimney, hearth and floor so clean appear;
The sweet smell of fresh linen and new cloathes,
The look of joyous glee each face so sweetly shews.

IV.

Brass, pewter, delf and tinware shining bright,
  New-furbish'd and arrang'd the night before;
The losset, dresser, chairs and tables white
    The level streetway swept before the door,
    Now from the press the mother brings her store—

The teapot black, on sundays only seen,
    With all his train—bowl, saucers, cups and ewer
Crown the brown parlor-table once again,
And butter'd to the core a smoking cake between.

V.

In a new face, clean, ruddy from the suds,
    Without his coat the father takes his chair,
A holy joy the good wife's feelings glad
    To see him still so healthy, strong and fair;
    With laughing, arch, blue eyes and curly hair,
His little favorite, seated on his knee,
    Of every dainty gets the largest share,
Who lisping, prattling, tells with infant glee
Of all he thro' the week had chanc'd to hear or see.

VI.

How yesternight he wander'd far away
    With sister Bessy going to the well,
How ploughman John detain'd her on the way,
    Beneath his great-coat while the shower fell,
    And gave him sixpence that he might not tell,

Abash'd and blushing with averted eyes,
   Poor Bess whose looks betray her heart too well,
The more to hide her sentiments she tries,
Reveals them yet the more, unpractis'd in disguise.

VII.

Loving and mild as on her bridal day,
   The happy mother frequently surveys
Her social household, innocently gay,
   And takes each opportunity to praise,
   Each child in turn, who blushing deep betrays
Their joy of joys in a pleas'd parent's smile,
   A cheering hope illumes her future days,
That these will shortly bear their parent's toil,
And the long vale of years with filial love beguile.

VIII.

The Cotter now his garden pacing slow,
   Along the sunny hedge beyond the stile.
His eldest boys behind him in a row
   Point out where they all week had plied their toil,
And each is bless'd with an approving smile,

For every plot is level, neat, and square,
No weeds the turnips, pears or onions soil,
   The flower edgings are all blooming fair,
But lo, the sundial white proclaims the hour of prayer.

IX.

Along the fringéd path in neat array
   Proceeding now they gain the mountain road,
Where many a kindly neighbour bids good day,
   Whom the sweet Sabbath only brings abroad
In whitish frieze which housewives most applaud,
And velvet collars are the youngsters seen;
   The lasses with trim caps and flounces broad,
Bright rockspun shawl and mitred pilareen,   [ween.
Shrinking from lover's gaze, tho' pleas'd therewith I

X.

Hail, holy Sabbath, day of peace and joy,
   All heaven and earth are harmony and love;
The very fields rejoice, and the deep sky
   So bright and blue invite our thoughts above;
A solemn silence reigns in field and grove,

Save when yon lonely ancient trees among
   The chiming bell each loiterer to reprove,
Calls from the hills around a happy throng,
Who in their best attire come lovingly along.

XI.

The old ones of the weather and the crops
   Hold converse deep and speculations wise,
The rise of bread before the years elapse,
   The farmer's hopes and Cotter's fear supplies;
And then the news of mingled truth and lies.
The sage remark : tithes, poor rates, and " repeal,"
   What taxes next will government devise ?
What did emancipation yet avail ?   [prevail ?
How stands affairs in France ?   How long will peace

XII.

The young ones, happy in their little joys,
   Make assignations for the afternoon,
In timid whispers, while averted eyes
   And blushes vainly check'd too well make known,
What artless modest maid would fain disown

While thrilling raptures agitate her mind,
    And many an anxious glance around is thrown,
Lest prying eyes observe them from behind;
But all alike engag'd, no time for watching find.

XIII.

Amidst these joyous groups *one* walks alone,
    Companionless, tho' fairest of the fair;
A settl'd grief in her sweet face is shewn,
    For pensive beauty loves to linger there,
    A mother, but unwed—now pale despair
Flings its cold shadow o'er her future years;
    How her heart freezes 'neath the scornful stare
Of former playmates, and in fancy hears
Sly whispers of the cause of all her sighs and tears!

XIV.

Around the ancient straw-clad house of prayer
    In melancholy musings now they go,
For of the living hundreds passing there,
    Not one but marks where some dear friend lies low,
    There, aged fathers to their children shew

The very sod that shortly o'er their graves
  Will grow as green when they lie sleeping low;
Here weeping widows pick the falling leaves,
As o'er her husband's dust each desolately grieves.

XV.

Now in the house and presence of his God,
  The happy Cotter and his children kneel,
Can Kings while thousands tremble at their nod
  More truly, exquisitely, happy feel,
  As with pure hearts together they appeal
In full assurance that their humble prayer
  Will at the Throne of Grace as far avail,
As if a coach and six had brought them there,
To loll on silken seats, and catch the vulgar stare.

XVI.

Here e'en amidst his orisons profound.
  The simple Cotter stealing from Above
To his dear little ones all kneeling there,
  So good, so innocent, a look of love;
  And prays devoutly that when these remove

From out his home their fate in life to try;
    They like himself may firm in virtue prove,
Leading a blameless life of quiet joy,
With neither grief or pain their progress to annoy.

XVII.

The Service o'er, now to their cheerful home,
    Returning by the pathway o'er the green ;
Far down the vale amid the golden broom,
    Low peeping thro' the hedgerow'd ash is seen
    Their straw-clad cottage with its windows green
And whitewash'd front, where at their social meal
    All sit them down so happy and so clean;
There, peace, content and innocence prevail,
And thus each Sunday finds the cottage in the vale.

XVIII.

Delightful scenes which mem'ry well supplies,
    When I beneath a loving father's care,
In sweet reality these rural joys,
    Alas not duly valued then, did share
    Ere yet thrown forth on this vain world of care,

With none to shield, direct, or stand between
   Me and misfortune, as when tempests tear
A bark safe shelter'd in some creek serene,
And flings her to the winds out on the howling main.

XIX.

Erin my own, my dear lov'd fatherland!
   Long may such scenes as these adorn thy vales,
And never more may discord's flaming brand
   Disturb the harmony that now prevails.
   But peace and plenty over hills and dales
Go hand in hand till cultivation's bloom,
   From highest hills perfume the evening gales;
And social happiness all hearts relume,
And each on Sunday morn enjoy a happy home.

DUNBINNE'S BRIDE.
An Irish Fairy Tale.

ADDRESSED TO MAJOR PORTEUS.

   If 'midst the busy world remains
     A vestige of those feelings dear
   To boyhood—then wilt thou my strains
     Of Erin's homes with pleasure hear.

   For who that heard his Irish nurse
     In childhood sing her Fairy lore,
   But loves thro' life the magic verse,
     That can these halcyon moods restore?

I.

TWAS Hallowe'en, a moonless night,
    We sat around the old hearthstone;
In Auburn cottage warm and bright,
    On the white walls the turf fire shone.

II.

The stack was rak'd, the hempseed sown,
    At supper Ellen found the ring,
The kail stalks pull'd, the worsted thrown
    The apple from the beam did swing.

III.

The cricket pip'd his evening song,
    The purring cat repos'd at ease
Beside old Nero stretch'd along,
    Indulging in the evening blaze.

IV.

The children round my mother stood,
    At length their teazing did prevail;
For each had promis'd to be good,
    If she would tell a fairy tale.

V.

She told us one, and vouch'd it true,
    For she herself remember'd well
The time, the place, the parties too,
    Tho' but a child when it befel.

VI.

Young Betsy was a lovely maid,
    Tall, blooming, fair, and seventeen,
And well could dance " the White Cockade "
    With James the Cooper on the green.

VII.

A comely youth he was and brave,
    Nor ghost nor fairy did he fear;
By haunted rath or new made grave,
    Would whistling pass with careless air.

VIII.

On Sunday evenings to the dance,
    When youngsters rambl'd down the green;
Betsy and James (no doubt 'twas chance,)
    There arm in arm were surely seen.

IX.

Young Betsy's was the blythest song,
    When milkmaids sought the dewy dale;
As saunt'ring home the furze among,
    The Cooper bore her milking pail.

X.

But when October evenings came,
    Poor Betsy's cheek was pale and wan;
And ere December fill'd the stream,
    Poor Betsy's hopes of life were gone.

XI.

She died as sinks to soft repose
    A gentle child, but o'er her came
No hue of death, for still the rose
    Was on her lips and cheeks the same!

XII.

Old women whisper'd at her wake,
    "This is not her! She has not died!
I knew the fairies would her take,
    That she may be Dunbinne's Bride.

XIII.

She is now in fairy land, I fear
    She may not rest in hallow'd ground;
We see but her resemblance here,
    No corpse would in her grave be found."

XIV.

With milkwhite wands and garlands gay,
    While rose the *caione* sweetly slow;
Her funeral passed in long array,
    And hands were wrung and tears did flow.

XV.

And Cooper James mov'd sadly there,
    No tear bedew'd his troubl'd eye;
Deeply absorb'd in silent prayer,
    And firm intent and purpose high.

XVI.

Resolv'd to search each mystic rite,
    Tradition, witchcraft, magic, all,
In life and death, by day and night,
    To free her from Dunbinne's thrall.

XVII.

That night when all in slumber lay,
    Alone amidst the silent dead ;
He from her grave remov'd the clay,
    And soon laid bare the coffin lid.

XVIII.

With trembling hands and eager eye,
    He sternly tore the lid away;
Then fell with one heart-piercing cry,
    There, there, the empty grave clothes lay !

XIX.

Half-shelter'd by Dunloman fort,
    In a low straw-clad dingy shed,
A red-hair'd wizzard from the North,
    Fill'd all the land with mystic dread.

XX.

Milk he restor'd to cows run dry,
  With charmèd threads cur'd elf-shot swine,
Repell'd the blight of evil-eye
  Told fortunes, and found stolen kine.

XXI.

Bridegrooms bewitch'd his power confess'd,
  Changlings restor'd increas'd his fame,
By stars nativities could cast,
  From cups and cards could husbands name.

XXII.

One night while wintry winds did roar,
  Poor Cooper James urg'd restless on,
Stood now within that cabin door,
  Before the wond'rous fairy man.

XXIII.

He told his tale and tearful cross'd
  With silver thrice the wizzard's hand;
Who stood in deep abstraction lost,
  His thoughts away in fairy land.

XXIV.

Then in a low deep organ tone,
  Thus came his words—"Now mark me well,
On St. John's eve be thou alone,
  At midnight where no mortals dwell.

XXV.

Nor bark of dog, nor house cock's crow,
  Nor human voices can be heard;
Where South a running stream doth flow,
  And fern plants grow along the sward.

XXVI.

That night just at the midnight hour
  These ferns will blossom,—then make sure,
While ripens quick each fragile flower,
  That you the precious seed procure.

XXVII.

The following Friday, when midnight
  Hangs awful over earth and main;
Array'd in new made garments white,
  Be at the ford of Auchelane.

XXVIII.

Strong be thy heart when o'er the stream,
    The fairy squadrons march in line;
There dress'd in green the maid you claim,
    Will ride before the Geraldine.

XXIX.

Right in her face the fernseed throw,
    Repeating thrice the Saviour's name,
Then hold her fast while lightning's glow,
    And thunders roar, and fairies scream.

XXX.

There should thy efforts be in vain,
    Defeated by more potent spell;
One chance for thee doth yet remain,
    If strength and courage bear thee well.

XXXI.

Deep in the Rock of Cashel lies,
    A cave five fathoms under ground,
The entrance hid from mortal eyes;
    Can but on Beltane eve be found.

XXXII.

There, long hath lain, without a stain,
    The arms which holy Cormac wore ;
Procure them, and on Hallowe'en,
    Prepare for Auchelane once more.

XXXIII.

By prayer and penance, shrive thy soul,
    Strong heart and dexterous hand be thine ;
No witchcraft can these arms control,
    No spell secure the Geraldine.

XXXIV.

The merry bonfire night had pass'd,
    But James by no one there was seen ;
Nor at the fair, on Tuesday last,
    Nor in his shop nor on the green.

XXXV.

They tried the corn sheaf on the lake (7)
    They search'd the waters all around ;
Each planting, copsewood, bog and brake,
    But Cooper James was never found.

XXXVI.

When Hallowe'en came round again,
   The village blacksmith sleeping sound;
Was call'd three times distinct and plain!
   He reach'd the window with a bound.

XXXVII.

And half dismay'd in deep surprise,
   There in the bright moon's trembling beams
Plainly perceiv'd before his eyes
   The long lamented Cooper James!

XXXVIII.

Well mounted on a coal black steed,
   With coat of mail and helmet bright,
And sword and shield such as we read
   In olden days of ancient knight.

XXXIX.

His words the blacksmith's heart did thrill—
   "Come lose no time, your fire procure;
To shoe this horse use all your skill,
   And see you make his footing sure.

XL.

This night his mettle must be tried,
   In combat with no mortal foe;
If I succeed, Dunbinne's bride
   Will then be mine for weal or woe.

XLI.

But if I fall, which Heaven forbid,
   To-morrow will appear quite plain ;
The troubl'd waters streak'd with blood,
   Along the ford of Auchelane.

XLII.

O then let those we once lov'd dear,
   Who haply yet repeat our names ;
Do all they can with mass and prayer,
   For Betsy and poor Cooper James."—

XLIII.

With the first beams of early morn
   To Auchelane the blacksmith hied ;
The deep rent banks were all uptorn
   And streaks of blood the waters dyed ! !

XLIV.

And numbers have been heard to say
    They saw the blood and footprints too ;
And ever to his dying day,
    The blacksmith swore the fact was true.

XLV.

And until Betsy's mother died,
    At midnight every hallowe'en,
Around her bed a form would glide,
    Resplendent as an Eastern Queen.

XLVI.

No more of James our tale recalls,
    Or when, or where, or how he died ;
But in Glengevlin's fairy halls,
    Poor Betsy is Dunbinne's bride.

XLVII.

At times she's seen on Hallowe'en,
    When twilight brings the evening star ;
Careering with the fairy train,
    Along the heights of Swadlinbar.

THE GREGORY DAY.

In the Irish Hedge Schools, St. Gregory's Day, March the 12th, was kept a holiday, the master and scholars holding a feast in the school-house.

DEAR me! what an improvement in the age,
　　Since first I conn'd the Primer's pictur'd page,
Taught by lame Jack of circumscrib'd renown,
The great Longinus of my native town.
Where 'midst the simple neighbours who but he
Could sound the depths of "Voster's Rule of Three,"
Engrave a Sundial—make a Patrick's cross,
And catechise the children after Mass.
Find the Moon's age correct by "Doogan's Rule,"
And prove each neighb'ring pedagogue a fool.
All Pastorini's prophecies recite,
Memorials, letters and petitions write,

And if his trembling hand misled the pen,
A glass of " Poteen " set him right again.
Long in the Belfast Almanack his name
Was known to all the bards of puzzling fame,
Where well sung praises, lent to be repay'd,
Was his who best his reader could mislead.
I see him now again, within his school
Demurely seated on his " creepy stool,"
With little old thin face and whiskers trig,
Too grey to match his olive-colour'd wig,
Short brown surtout, and neatly mended hose,
Black cravat, buckskin, breeks and buckl'd shoes:—
And while he hears each pupil con his task,
Swig glorious mouthfuls from his poteen flask,
Enabl'd thus by sipping now and then
To nib a " large-hand " or a " small-hand " pen;
With one eye to the door, to ascertain
What brat neglected his " two turf" again.

   The crowded Atheneum scant of light,
By day a schoolhouse, but a byre by night;
There halfway up the floor, encircling round

Some smoky coals on the uneven ground,
The palefac'd blue-lipp'd ragged urchins throng,
The weak kept hindmost by the bold and strong,
Who dearly buy the heat which it supplies,
With speckl'd shins, kicks, cuffs and bleared eyes,
On logs of black bog-oak or piles of stone,
And round straw mats the rest promiscuous shone,
From tables, desks and all such lumber free,
Each scrawl'd his shapeless copy on his knee.

Now comes the long expected "Gregory Day,"
Devoted still to banqueting and play,
Each gives his mite, but whosoever bring
Most cash or whiskey will be crown'd "The King."

Ambition thou, great spur of men and gods,
How dost thou sometimes choose such mean abodes!
Each purse-proud mother who can scarcely tell
Her name in English, why wilt thou impel,
With silver to supply her booby son,
Lest by some neighbour-child the crown be won?
Thus halfpence, "tenpennies" and halfcrowns rise,
A glorious sight to Jack's delighted eyes;

While those of humbler views who deem it vain,
To try the proud distinction to obtain :
Eggs, butter, cream or oaten bannock bring,
And thus find access to the banqueting.

With jar of mountain poteen on his knee.
The master sits, and who so bless'd as he.
Nor had the wanton Paris ever press'd.
The Spartan queen more fondly to his breast ;
Than Jack his jar, the " taws" are thrown away,
And school-boys wonder he's so blythe and gay.
The egg-shells round, in lieu of glasses go.
Behind the tides of talk and laughter flow :
The master talks, and drinks and talks again,
And rises to a yet sublimer strain ;
Displays his mighty stock of bookish lore,
Tells all he ever knew, and owns to more.
Of grammar, ungrammatically speaks.
Describing rules, his every sentence breaks;
Recounts again, what words profound and long,
He us'd the day he prov'd the 'swadler' wrong,
Tells his high conversations with the priest.

Then spouts away at Alexander's feast,
" T'was at the royal feast *by* Persia won,"
"(Not *by* but *for*), by Philip's warlike son,"
Fir'd with the theme, and startling up to be,
In proper altitude—lo! from his knee,
Drops the forgotten jar,—that downward rolls,
To splinters smash'd among the flaming coals ;
The ignited poteen, rising fierce and high,
Wrapt all in flames, the boys too throng'd to fly,
Shins, legs, and eyebrows scorch'd, are headlong pil'd,
Others with blazing clothes and heads run wild ;
For loss and damages, and want of bail,
Poor limping Jack long linger'd in a jail ;
And thus broke up the school, where first I knew,
That a pen's track, could tell a tale so true.

LITTLE PORA,
A Domestic Irish Tale.

I.

A COMELY youth was Allen Roe,
    But he must go beyond the sea;
His mind to store with classic lore,
    That he a holy priest may be.

II.

And he hath look'd his last for years,
    On scenes more dear than ever now;
His father cheers his boyish fears,
    His mother's tears are on his brow.

III.

Down the old path and o'er the stile,
    They watch him in the morning sun
Along the hedge, beyond the height,
    He's out of sight—poor Allen's gone

IV.

His way should be across the lea,
    Then why along the Milldam go?
What is to him the miller's niece?
    No human love must Allen know.

V.

But little Dora smil'd so sweet,
    And they were both so very young,
Shall he not bid one kind adieu,
    A childish wish it can't be wrong.

VI.

In converse low away they go,
    Beyond the stile, the lane, the pool,
The poplar hedge, the broken bridge,
    Where they in childhood went to school.

VII.

And many a scene of joy serene
    These valleys green can now recall,
Here did they float their tiny boat,
    And watch'd it down the waterfall.

VIII.

Here oft at "Highgates" had they play'd,
    When noon releas'd them from their desk,
There join'd the play of "hound and hare,"
    Together here rehears'd their task.

IX.

There many a baby house they built,
    With daisies pil'd for baby beds;
There nestl'd from the summer rain,
    Their little bibs about their heads.

X.

But she must fly, the miller calls,
    I know not if they kiss'd at parting;
But little Dora's eyes were red,
    Though all her playfulness exerting.

XI.

Her grief to hide—but tears denied
    Her pining heart did more consume;
For ever fraught with one sad thought:
    "He 'll be a priest when he comes home."

XII.

Old time flies fast, ten years are pass'd,
  And home at last came Allen Roe;
A priest of God, tall, pale, and sad,
  Few would in him the schoolboy know.

XIII.

It was a summer Sunday morning,
  Birds were warbling everywhere;
Dewdrops from the springing corn,
  Rose like golden mists in air.

XIV.

In their best all gaily dress'd,
  O'er valley, meadow, stile, and pass;
Came the whole Parish on that day,
  For Father Allen will give mass.

XV.

How throb'd poor little Dora's heart,
  Too young and artless to conceal
Her hopes and fears, now full to tears,
  Now blushing deep, now deadly pale.

XVI.

Trembling and faint, she nestl'd down,
    At once inside the chapel door;
And pray'd for grace—but Oh! that face,
    May she not gaze on it once more.

XVII.

"Intriho ad altare Dei,"
    What solemn sounds! a quivering thrill
Runs thro' her blood to that lov'd voice,
    Her heart replied against her will.

XVIII.

Caught by surprise she rais'd her eyes,
    The golden light of morning gleams
On that pale, melancholy face,
    For ever present in her dreams.

XIX.

She cannot raise her thoughts to heaven,
    She reads her litanies in vain;
Invoking blessed Mary's aid,
    She cannot help but look again.

XX.

Alas for Dora's sinful soul,
  Oh! can she ever be forgiven;
Thus kneeling in the house of God,
  To love the anointed priest of heaven!

XXI.

That night she wept while others slept,
  With morning knelt in silent prayer,
Alas for woman's faithful heart,
  Young Allen's image still was there.

XXII.

There is a lake in Donegal (8)
  Far westward many a weary mile,
'Mid naked hills and dreary moors,
  There lies St. Patrick's holy isle.

XXIII.

There pilgrims come for nine long days,
  And wakeful nights to fast and pray;
That thus by penitence and prayer,
  Their sins may all be wash'd away.

XXIV.

There as with unremitting care,
  The Prior went his nightly round,
To see that all shall watch and pray,
  One lay extended on the ground.

XXV.

He sternly call'd but call'd in vain,
  A Sister rais'd her drooping head ;
The gentle pilgrim wakes no more,
  Poor little Dora there lay dead !

XXVI.

I know a graveyard far away,
  Beside a lonely little hill ;
Where nettles grow by headstones low,
  And four old yew trees linger still.

XXVII.

Close by the ivy'd old Church wall,
  Between two hawthorns bending low,
A grave is seen, smooth, round and green,
  Where daffodils and violets grow.

XXVIII.

At midnight there in silent prayer,
   Was frequent seen, by one who knew
Poor Allen Roe, on Dora's grave,
   A grey old man at thirty-two.

XXIX.

And every Sunday till he died,
   (The de profundis ended slow,)
He asked a prayer from all knelt there,
   For one whose name he whisper'd low.

LINES WRITTEN ON JANUARY 1st, 1849.

IT was the "witching hour of night,"
  When ghosts and fairies take delight
In fright'ning men; and coffin lids
Uprais'd, exhibit ghastly heads;
And witches chaunting runic rhymes
On broomsticks, fly to distant climes.
Just as that chancelor of time,
The old church clock, proclaim'd the chime
Of midnight near, an old man came
Up from the west, thin, bald, and lame;
His nose and chin were nearly met,
His piercing eyeballs deeply set
'Neath furrow'd brows with curves impress'd,
A length of beard hung down his breast,
As o'er the far blue realms of light
He swept along with rapid flight,
A darkling cloud still hung before,
Behind a mist of floating hoar,

Thro' which at intervals was seen
Ruins of things that once had been;
And wheresoe'er a look he cast,
All things shrunk with'ring as he pass'd.
'Twas father Time, th' insatiate foe
Of all things beautiful below;
As near this whirling world he pass'd,
Thus rose his voice above the blast :
"Well there you lie, old Forty-eight,
Another hour decides your fate;
Your breath is short, your voice is low,
Your nose is pinch'd, your pulse is slow;
And there you gasp, in mortal strife,
The relics of a misspent life.
Like old Erastratus, your name
Shall live in execrable fame,
An epoch for remarks and dates,
In chronological debates.
Now wretch, unfaithful to your charge,
Look round this shatter'd world at large,
See to what ruin things are driven,

LINES WRITTEN ON JANUARY 1ST, 1849.

Since you succeeded Forty-seven;
In France is neither king or throne,
The Bourbons all to exile flown;
The Prussian tott'ring to his fall,
The Pope evicted bulls and all,
Imperial Austria crownless driven,
Negociates now a peace with Heaven.
Frankfort, Palermo, and Madrid,
Like seething pot, boil o'er the lid ;
Constantinople and New York,
Half roasted by your scoundrel work,
The fainting Mexican yet bleeds,
The hardy Switzers fight for creeds,
View Creoles, Kaffirs, Sikhs, and Poles,
Still glow like half extinguish'd coals ;
Nay e'en John Bull, in dudgeon fumes,
O'er smithies cold, and idle looms,
And Pat depriv'd of his potatoes;
Intractable as old Prometheus,
Swears tho' he perish in a jail,
His dying shout shall be " repeal."

In short where'er I look around,
Are traces of your mischief found ;
Go, wretch, and may your like again,
Ne'er usurp the annual reign."
The clock strikes twelve, the old man dies.
And down from th' Empyrean skies,
A youth descending takes his place,
Bright hope depicted in his face;
Like organ-tones in vaulted fane
The voice of Time was heard again:
"Be thine, young man, with filial care
Thy sire's misconduct to repair.
In realms convuls'd with dark intrigues,
Treason and war, with all their plagues—
Bid order, peace and plenty smile
As in yon favour'd sea-girt Isle,
Where commerce, wealth, industry, power,
And wisdom are fair Freedom's dower."
Old Time rush'd on, the youth pursued,
And up the arch of Heaven strode.
To-day he first attempts the Line,
And mortals call him " Forty-nine."

FRANTIC MARY,

A Tale Founded on Fact.

AS dew-drench'd rose was Mary's lip,
    With amber locks o'er eyes of blue,
And playful as the lambs that sip
The mountain dew would Mary trip,
    While sung the lone cuckoo.

II.

Well did I know her mother's cot,
    High on the sloping woodland side;
The winding lane, the clover plot,
The straggling hedge, the cow boy's hut,
    Down by the Camlin side.

III.

And well I knew the primrose bank,
  Deep shelter'd in the vale below ;
Where oft the milkmaid's treat I drank,
And help'd her o'er the bending plank;
  As homeward she did go.

IV.

And fondly yet my heart retains,
  The air of every plaintive song,
She thrill'd so sweet as o'er the plains,
The evening breezes bore the strains
  That to her cows she sung.

V.

How well these cows had learn'd to know,
  And love her songs 'twas plain to see ;
Chewing the cud so still, so slow,
As frisking their tails, with grateful low,
  They gave their milk more free.

VI.

In yonder glen at eventide,
   When dancers tripp'd the daisied green;
Bless'd was the youth who with her tried,
The mazy " reel," or by her side,
   Could steal a glance unseen.

VII.

Then Edward shar'd the fair one's smile,
   With him she linger'd on the dew;
Along the paths by gate and stile,
When ev'ning bells releas'd from toil,
   To whisper love they flew.

VIII.

At pathron dance, wake, ball or fair,
   On Sundays by the mountain grove;
The fondest, fairest, happiest pair,
Was Edward and his Mary there,
   Indulging dreams of love.

FRANTIC MARY.

IX.

When winter nights were dark and long,
    And circl'd round the fairy tale ;
Among the cheerful careless throng,
'Twas sweet to hear her homely song,
    As merrily went the wheel.

X.

A squire came o'er the limekiln Brea,
    As Mary sat by the cooling spring,
His eyes were bright, his dress was gay,
He talk'd of love till near mid-day,
    And parting gave a ring.

XI.

He came again o'er the limekiln Brea,
    When evening hung on the mountain lone,
He led poor Mary's soul astray,
He led poor Mary far away,
    Thro' ways to her unknown.

XII.

They pass'd the rath where fairies hide,
   The haunted mill, the graveyard green,
The bridle road, where on each side,
The wood-quests ominously cried
   In copse-wood shades unseen.

XIII.

Onward they sped as the night grew dark;
   Silent and solemn was all around,
Save far away the housedog's bark,
The corncreak's notes in the bearded park,
   And falling waters sound.

XIV.

Where o'er yon shingl'd roof tree tall,
   An ancient oak the storm defies;
As whistles the wind thro' the dreamy hall,
And twinkles the shadows along the wall,
   There Mary sits and sighs.

XV.

Her faithless squire his smiles forbore,
  No priest had bless'd their bridal bed ;
For her the dream of life was o'er,
On her, content, must smile no more,
  Her bloom, her spirits fled.

XVI.

Alas! how chang'd:—In speechless woe
  A thin pale hand her cheek did press;
Swaying convulsively to and fro,
While scalding tears, round, full and slow,
  Dropt on her faded dress.

XVII.

Her thoughts were of her comrades fair,
  Still cheerful, innocent, pure and free;
With gladsome hopes from year to year,
And faithful swains who lov'd them dear,
  And still would faithful be.

XVIII.

The summer Sunday evenings fine,
    The jocund youngsters all abroad;
Love link'd in pairs, she sees them twine
Their hands in play a smiling line,
    Along Clonbroney road.

XIX.

The winter nights, the shining hearth,
    The games, the forfeits, jokes and songs,
The whisper'd vows, the hearty mirth,
Which she no more can share on earth,
    Tho' yet so fair and young.

XX.

Never must she behold them more,
    The mark of shame is on her brow;
The good and pure could but deplore;
Her Edward too—Oh! hers no more,
    All, all despis'd her now.

XXI.

Never again, O never more
   Can she rejoin that cheerful throng;
Her hopes, her joys, her peace is o'er;
Her Edward—wildly on the floor
   Her wasted form she flung.

XXII.

She wander'd sad by dawn of day,
   Along the lonely Camlin side
Recumbent on the new-mown hay,
With folded hands did kneeling pray,
   Then jump'd into the tide.

XXIII.

A herdsman saw the fearful deed,
   And plunging bore her to the shore,
His care recall'd her from the dead,
But, O! the lamp of Reason shed,
   Its guiding light no more.

XXIV.

The sun had sunk in the hazy west,
    The winds were loud in the mountain caves,
When Mary return'd so thinly dress'd,
But the palor of death did her brow invest,
    As she sat midst the falling leaves.

XXV.

Her eyes were dim, her lips were blue,
    She sung a low, sweet wailing song,
But screaming wild, to the brakes withdrew,
As whining with joy to her bosom flew
    The dog she had lov'd so long.

XXVI.

And if her parent came in view,
    Starting, she flew to the leafy dells,
Wander'd all day o'er the mountains blue,
And slept at night in the cold grey dew,
    Among the heather bells.

XXVII.

And once a farmer pacing round,
  His orchard fruit from thieves to save,
In the adjoining grave-yard found,
Poor frantic Mary sleeping sound,
  Across her father's grave.

XXVIII.

She sat by the spring at twilight dim,
  Leaning her cheek on her wasted hand,
When nearer came—no dreaming whim,
Her Edward—yes—O, yes, 'tis *him*,
  Who o'er her now doth stand.

XXIX.

Fast fell his tears on her tangl'd hair,
  With thoughts of happier days oppress'd,
His Mary once, so pure, so fair,
No longer could the youth forbear,
  He snatch'd her to his breast.

XXX.

Around his neck her arms she flung,
 In piercing shrieks of wild despair,
He felt her heart with anguish wrung,
As screaming from his grasp she sprung,
 Across the hills afar.

XXXI.

Never was Mary seen again
 Her native fields and haunts among,
And some averr'd they had seen quite plain,
Her ghost where winds the shaded lane,
 With boortrees overhung.

XXXII.

Her mother in fierce distraction wild,
 On bare bent knees his door beside,
Curs'd the seducer of her child;
He shrieking fled, by all revil'd,
 And in a madhouse died.

XXXIII.

Some rankling weeds now mark the spot,
    Where Mary once in beauty's bloom,
Spread joy around her mother's cot,
And still they sing her hapless lot
    In many a mountain home.

THE SHEEBEEN HOUSE.

I.

REMEMBER you the Sheebeen House,
   By the bridle road behind the Mill,
The scene of many a deep carouse,
   Within my mind I view it still,
   The rank green pool, the lazy rill,
Bridg'd by the smooth worn old millstone,
   The mudwall front, the hollow roof,
   The boarded chimney slop'd aloof,
The thatch with weeds o'er grown,
   The rugged streetway duly brush'd,
The night before the fair,
   The batter'd window thick with dust,
And ever and always there
Peep'd through one patch'd-up pane (the next a rag in)
A broken jug, lame glass, and dinted naggin.

II.

I am now within the sheebeen house,
    Where oftentimes I've sat before,
The grey cat lists the nibbling mouse,
    In the old chest behind the door,
    The sunbeams on the puddl'd floor,
Reflected round the smoky walls,
    The old black pipe is on the hob,
    The old wife at her weary job,
Where round two smouldering coals,
    The dusty mill-seeds darkly glow;
There on her creepy stool,
    Her spinning wheel revolving slow,
    She feeds the humming spool;
And ever as her work goes well, betrays
In scrap of lively song, her fire of younger days.

III.

I see her broad, brown chubby face,
    Her dappl'd tete and furrow'd brow;
Still in her large grey eyes I trace,

Feelings her years might disavow;
The red serge gown, I see it now,
The dunn old cap and kerchief blue,
The linsey petticoat half brac'd,
Around her clumsy, shapeless waist,
Her apron never new.
Behind the grey partition wall,
And bleak brown dresser bare,
In a safe nook conceal'd from all,
Stood the big-bellied jar;
Behind that daily couch and nightly bed,
Where many a courting pair forgot how time had sped.

IV.

On winter nights a little lad,
There seated on the creepy stool,
I lov'd to hear the laughter glad,
The song, the jest and ridicule,
But often to a corner stole,
When fiercely rag'd the drunken row,
The lights blown out, the tables smash'd,

THE SHEEBEEN HOUSE.

 Pots, jugs and stools at random cast,
And many a swollen brow,
 And broken nose and batter'd head,
Reveal'd the fearful fray.
 When careful of the unwash'd blood
 On face and clothes for proof—they stood
Before the court next day,
Where cravens to repay their drubbings loth,
Plac'd all their hopes of vengeance in an oath.

v.

And when black John the feather man,
 At nightfall slily came alone,
He always some strange lie could plan
 That soon induc'd me to be gone;
 His motive then to me unknown,
I well could guess in after days,
 I wish I were as artless yet,
 Tho' thro' this world thereby less fit
To steer my weary ways;
 But dearly is such knowledge bought,

And delicate the line,
   'Twixt vice and worldly wisdom sought,
As in the labour'd mine.
The richest strata to the miner's hand   [sand.
Gives with one grain of ore a thousand grains of

VI.

I see her daughter, little Bess,
   She was in sooth a bonny child;
Who was her father none might guess,
   But archly little Bessy smil'd,
   Fresh as a morning rose unsoil'd;
Her crimson lip and blushing cheek;
   And witchingly of love and joy,
   And stolen hearts her gipsy eye
Could eloquently speak;
   And many a youngster came to woo
In bashful tenderness;
   And deeply quaff'd the "mountain dew"
While courting little Bess;
Whose blooming beauty rumour'd near and far,
Drew ample custom to her mother's jar.

THE SHEEBEEN HOUSE.

VII.

The Sheebeen wife increas'd her gains,
    But bonny Bessy's bloom declin'd;
Gone were her glad light-hearted strains,
    Some secret grief oppress'd her mind,
    Inconstant as the veering wind;
Her lovers vanish'd one by one,
    Poor Bessy and her mother's jar
    The livelong night neglected were,
Lovers and topers gone;
    Poor Bessy lies in yon churchyard,
Dying she gave another birth;
    No more through falling floods is heard
    The frequent roars of drunken mirth;
The Sheebeen house attracts the eye no more,
The hostess begs her bread from door to door.

MY ONCE HAPPY HOME.

I.

WHY pensively still do I visit this valley,
    Why linger my steps by each meadow and
stream,
And mem'ry o'er shaded with deep melancholy,
    Recall other days like the light of a dream?
Tho' simple these uplands and homely these flowers,
    Tho' solitude broods o'er the fields where I roam,
Yet, ah! 'tis the scene of my juvenile hours,
    The ruin'd remains of my once happy home.

II.

Deep voices encumber the wind as it passes,
    And talk of the blessings of years fled away,
When happy enjoying a father's caresses
    I play'd by his knee on each fine sabbath day.
Along the close hedges with rowan trees shaded,
    He led my young mind o'er past ages to roam
In history's volumes whose wonders pervaded
    My innocent mind in my once happy home.

III.

And here stood the cottage where joyance resided,
   Its windows half seen thro' the trees in a row,
Along its thatch'd eaves the big shower-drops glided,
   Quick pattering on the broad burdocks below
The streamlet in June lost in winding meanders
   That loud thro' the winter would thundering foam,
Where dreaming awake in the twilight I've wander'd
   When summer surrounded my once happy home.

IV.

There once bloom'd the garden with boortrees surrounded,
   And there was the well with its streamlet so clear;
The hawthorn stood there with green benches around it,
   The haunt of the cuckoo when summer was near,
The weed fringéd pathway you upland ascending,
   Where evening hath often involv'd me in gloom,
Observing the hills with the dark vapours blending
   And white mists surrounding my once happy home.

V.

Conceal'd in the shade of these tall waving rushes,
    O'er Thomson and Goldsmith I've por'd with delight,
Or to a proud father among the furze bushes,
    My first simple verses from mem'ry recite.
Oft since in my dreams, when at distance I wander,
    These scenes to my lone heart at midnight will come,
And features long wasted the grey head stone under
    Salute me again in my once happy home.

VI.

In the pathway of life tho' I've since tasted pleasure,
    And kind hearts have prais'd my untunable song,
Contentment and health have to me been a treasure,
    And joy lent a smile as I travell'd along;
But fate has no gift in her earthly possessions,
    Tho' health, peace, and plenty attend to the tomb
To equal the raptures of childish impressions,
    The innocent joys of our first happy home.

TO THE RIGHT HONOURABLE VISCOUNT PALMERSTON,

On his Eightieth birth day, Oct. 20th, 1864.

WHILE bards of tenhorse power, who've got
    Their M.A.'s, L.D.'s, and all that,
In pompous pedantry display
Their piles of birth-day odes to-day,
May I attempt with reverence due
To say my say among them too;
In cheerful strains such as befit
The man whose genius, wisdom, wit,
And wondrous energy appears
Now at the end of Eighty years;
More active, fresh, and buoyant than
Others can show at twenty-one;

And with so many years gone by
Still more inclin'd to laugh than cry.
No hiding of remorseful fears
Beneath th' excuse of cank'ring years,
But calmly, cheerful as beseems
A well-spent lifetime's evening beams.
   Hail wondrous Nestor of our age,
What shifting scenes have cross'd the stage
Of life since Broadland's woods and skies
Smil'd on thy childhood's artless joys.
Four sov'reigns on the English throne
Erin and Albion join'd as one;
Old Greece recover'd, Poland gone,
Columbia lost, Hindostan won;
New Zealand and Australia founded,
The Nile trac'd up, the North pole rounded;
Reform, Free Trade, Emancipation,
Blest Homœopathic renovation,
Phrenology to shew at once
If John o' Stiles be knave or dunce;

Gas, Photography, Locomotion,
Missives convey'd beneath the ocean;
Napoleon and the Bourbons gone,
Prince Albert, Nelson, Wellington,
Pitt, Chatham, Eldon, Castlereagh,
Fox, Burke, and Canning pass'd away;
Peel, Erskine, Cobbett, Arkwright, Watt,
Moore, Byron, Sheridan, and Scott,
Like meteors swept across the sky,
They come, ascend, blaze out, and die.

If Atlas gain'd, as poets say,
Such glory that he for one day
Bore up the world, how vast thy fame,
Who fifty years have done the same.
Thro' all those years, O what a strain
On that invulnerable brain!
O what a world of thought have sped
Thro' that o'erburden'd, weary head!
Yet it is still as cool and clear
As if renew'd each coming year;

Long may'st thou yet the rudder guide,
Secure with fav'ring wind and tide;
For wert thou gone, O what a tussle
With Whigs and Tories in a bustle!
Scrambling and hauling, all pell mell,
To catch thy mantle as it fell.

A DREAM OF YOUTH.

Air—*Nancy Neal.*

IN sleep a dream possess'd my mind,
    I found myself once more
Among the lonely glens reclin'd
    My youth had wander'd o'er.
The linnet, thrush, and woodlark nigh
    On mountain grove and plain,
Awoke a thrilling song of joy
    To welcome me again.

My father press'd his own green seat
    Beneath the alder tree,
And smil'd I could so well repeat
    My lesson at his knee.
My mother o'er her milking pail
    Down in the shelter'd lane,
Sung each sweet song that I so long
    Had pin'd to hear again.

A DREAM OF YOUTH.

The moon was on the mountain brow,
    The mist was on the hill,
Around the bright hearth blazing now
    Each their old place did fill.
Fond brothers laugh'd while at her wheel,
    Each sister join'd the strain,
Then deeply, sweetly did I feel
    My heart at home again.

The freshness of my youth came back,
    My heart was young once more,
Forgetful of each weary track
    In life I'd wander'd o'er;
But soon, alas, my dream was flown,
    Awake to care and pain,
I found my weary soul alone,
    Far, far from home again!

MY SUMMER DAYS ARE OVER.

AIR—*Leading the Calves.*

NOW sixty-four eventful years
    Have swept o'er earth and ocean,
Since first this half extinguish'd heart
    Awoke to life and motion.
Since then what change of sun and shade
    My horoscope did cover,
But night comes on, I'll soon be gone,
    My summer days are over.

O, might I but recall again
    The sunny scenes of childhood
And re-enjoy my boyish years
    Like the lark in leafy wood!
The morning glow of long ago,
    Could I again recover;
But why complain, 'tis all in vain,
    My summer days are over.

MY SUMMER DAYS ARE OVER.

When dark October moans along
    The naked hill and valley,
I sadly watch the evening sun
    In pensive melancholy,
To think these trees and wither'd fields
    Their verdure will recover;
But youth once o'er comes back no more,
    And mine, alas, is over.

Yet, tho' the hoary tinge of years
    Is o'er my temples stealing,
Tho' day by day departs for aye
    Some dear long cherish'd feeling.
Old friends to meet and warmly greet,
    Can vanish'd joys recover,
Till even yet I half forget
    That my summer days are over.

THE HOME I LEFT BEHIND.

Air.—On Board the Victory.

AN Irish maiden sat alone by Susquehana shore,
    Reposing from the weary miles she'd lately wander'd o'er,
So sadly, sweetly, low she sung, while falling tears did blind,
And still the burden of her song, was the home I left behind.

Now summer smiles in Erin's Isle, on hills and vallies gay,
Where my contented playmates all together sport and play ;
The milkmaid's song now floats along the perfume laden wind,
And woodbines blow and daisies grow round the home I left behind.

Next Sunday at the evening dance, will lads and lasses throng,

Then homeward ramble hand in hand, the winding lanes among ;
But I must join their sports no more, nor ever, ever find,
My heart at rest on some fond breast, in the home I left behind.
It was a dreary winter day, the snow lay on the moor,
When landlord, bailiffs, and police broke in our cottage door ;
They drove my widow'd mother forth, but death to her was kind,
She sleeps beside my father near the home I left behind.

And now I wander, sad and lone, among these prairies wild,
Still dreaming o'er each happy scene that bless'd me when a child.
Cold strangers heedless mark my tears, but never can I find
The friendly smile of my own green isle in the home I left behind.

TRANSLATION OF "TIR NA HOIGDHE,"

By Loras Ceiocu.

O COULD I persuade my young fair one to follow
    To the mountains of Sligo away,
On fleet steeds well mounted, far far from this valley
    We would fly ere the dawning of day.
        For parents or kindred our absence bewailing
        How little we'd care o'er the broad Shannon sailing,
        In the vales of the west our raptures concealing,
        We would love until time was no more.

If the fates were so kind to transport us together
    To that island recorded in song,
Where youth is perpetual, and hearts never wither,
    But each year find us blooming and young.
        Together we'd stay there for ages delighted,
        And time rolling by find our hearts more united,
        For that fair hand I'd know when by thousands invited*
        And we'd love until time was no more.

* This alludes to a kind of marriage by lot at the great Fair of Talthean, where the young women thrust each a finger through a perforated partition, which hid them from view, when the young men each seized a finger, and was obliged to marry the owner.

ELLEEN A ROON,

Rendered literally from Carroll O'Daly's original song.

I'D leave house and hall with you, Elleen a Roon,
    Thro' deep woods I'd stroll with you, Elleen a Roon.
Your calves gently calling,
We'd lead them forth all the way,
Down to Tyrawley, dear Elleen a Roon.

Will you fly away with me, Elleen a Roon?
Will you now fly away with me, Elleen a Roon?
Will you now fly away with me,
Your promise I claim from you,
Or am I deceiv'd by you, Elleen a Roon?

A hundred thousand welcomes, Elleen a Roon,
A hundred thousand welcomes, Elleen a Roon;
A hundred thousand welcomes,
With your locks wreath'd brightly,
My lasting delight shall be—Elleen a Roon.

THE ORIGINAL COOLIN.

AN CHU'ILIN.
(County Cavan Dialect.)

A Chuilín ua 'n oir fult, na pós thusa an striol;
Neamhighcon a chuid boilach 's oir chiste an t-saoghal,
Nach m-bearr duitsa oig-fhear ag do phoigui gach trian,
No sebhris Righ na Foila do chroignui faoi chian.

A chuisle mo chroidhe sti an dtiucfuidh choidhche an lae,
An a mbeidh mise agus tu féin air an inntis a-bhan,
An glas air an dorus agus an eochair air iaridh,
Agus cuig mhile ponte air an unsa do 'n iaran.

TRANSLATION.*

MY golden hair'd Coolin, do not wed that boor,
Tho' large be his flocks, and abundant his store,
More blest the endearment Love's mornings bestow,
Than misers recounting their treasures can know.

Dear pulse of my heart will the evening e'er come,
That we both together shall dwell in one home,
The door lock'd securely no key to be found,
And one ounce of iron cost five thousand pounds?

* This is a strictly literal translation of two verses of that well-known song "The Coolin," which I have heard my mother often sing at her spinning wheel, in the original Irish. It is

NOTES.

Page 7 (1) See Byron's description of the Dying Gladiator; Childe Harold, canto 4th.

Page 8 (2) The "Horn of Plenty" in the heathen mythology in allusion to the encouragement always given by His Royal Highness to the study of agriculture.

Page 14 (4) Sir Humphrey Chetham, founder of the celebrated Manchester Library; John Byrom, who first established the weaving trade extensively in Manchester and the adjoining villages; the celebrated Dr. Dee, whose unenviable notoriety as a wizard made some noise in Lancashire, was contemporary with Bishop Oldham, who endowed the Free Grammar School; John Earl De le Warre was the founder of the Old Collegiate Church.

Page 35 (5) The scenery of this poem I have copied from real life in Ireland, such as it was in the days of my childhood before the commencement of that agitation which resulted in returning a few Roman Catholic members to parliament, and at the same time sacrificed thousands upon thousands of forty shilling freeholders, who were soon evicted, their happy homes broken up, and the inmates driven to wander over the earth. Thence commenced that fearful system of depopulation that has changed

---

the simple address of a lover to his beloved, and contains no allusion whatever to politics or coercion as stated by Walker in his Irish Bards, and after him by Moore in the Irish Melodies.

Ireland into a wilderness; and that fearful rush of emigration which still continues, and which, notwithstanding the recent speeching to the contrary, leaves Ireland poorer and weaker. A few rich graziers shew very well at an agricultural dinner, but where are the hardy stalworth thousands that help'd to win the battles of Busaco, Vimeira, Gwallior, and Waterloo, truly did poor Oliver Goldsmith write :—

> Ill fares the land to hastening ills a prey,
> Where wealth accumulates and men decay.

Page 45 Of the many relics of the olden time found among the Irish of the present day, the belief in the existence of fairies is held up as the strongest proof of their ignorance and superstition, yet it would not be difficult to prove that this old belief is on the contrary a proof of the love of justice and the spirit of inquiry of our forefathers.

Before the introduction of Christianity into Ireland, the religion was druidism, and the ceremonies practised by the Irish druids was with slight and incidental alterations the same as that given to the Persians by Zoroaster, and the fire-temples of the guebers are almost similar to the clactheachs or round towers of which moderns have written so much and know so little.

The Irish druids like the Persians had their places of worship in consecrated groves on "sacred hills" or by "holy wells."

There they taught the people, and exhorted them to the practice of virtue and morality. They believed in the immortality and transmigration of souls, and in an Almighty Deity, whose dwelling place was in the sun, and whom they called Baal or Belus.

This god they honoured with fires and festivals at the vernal and autumnal equinoxes, which custom has come down to the present day in the fires kindled on all the hills on midsummer's eve. On May eve, a fire was kindled in honour of Baal, "The bright god," that the days might be sunny and warm, and the flocks and pastures thrive; and the day is still named in the Irish language Labaaltenne *i.e.* the day of Baal's fire.

Another great festival was held on the last eve of October, in honour of Samhin or the Black god, that the nights throughout the winter might be bright and clear; and hence it is that we keep up the festival of hallow's eve with all its ceremonies of divination, fortune telling, snatch apple, &c.

Like other eastern nations, the ancient Irish had also the terrible custom of offering up human victims on these occasions.

There is a high hill called Usnach, in the county of Westmeath, near Kinnegad. This hill was formerly called "The Navel of Ireland," because the five provinces met there.

On that hill, at stated periods, the monarch, the arch-druid, and the chief *brehons* met to revise, promulgate, and execute the laws. There such as had been guilty of certain crimes were publicly tried and sentenced to die—on the dread night of the festival of Samhin, when all the condemned criminals were taken to a place in the county of Leitrim, called Maghsleachta, or "The Field of Slaughter." It was a deep, dark valley, in the centre of a gloomy wood of oaks, where had stood for ages till destroyed by St. Patrick, a black rough stone pillar, rudely shaped into a fierce and terrible form, and was called Crum Cruach; twelve smaller pillars stood round, forming a circle of which Crum Cruach was the centre.

Inside this circle were erected two huge figures, in imitation of the human form, made of stakes and wicker work; into these were hurled all the criminals indiscriminately, when the two frames were set on fire and consumed, with all their living contents, amidst the agonising shrieks, screams, and yells of the wretched victims, and the hideous shouts and cheers of the surrounding multitude.

Besides the two great festivals of Baltenne and Samhin, there were two others dividing the year into four quarters, or as the Irish have it, Ratha, and these also are still kept up as Candlemasday and Luinisa on the first of August.

Moore, in his history of Ireland, observes, that in no country in Europe did the first Christian missionaries make such extensive concessions to the traditions and ceremonies of the Pagans as in Ireland. So that these four great festivals are still observed, simply dedicated to certain saints since they could not suppress them, and because they could not find the particular birth or death of any saint falling on the great festival of Samhin, they dedicated the day to "All Saints," while at the same time the "Sacred hills" and "Holy wells" are still frequented, having been dedicated to certain saints by the early missionaries for the same reason.

But to come more directly to the origin of fairies in Ireland, when St. Patrick preached the Gospel to the Irish he was, as is well known, received with hospitality and kindness, instead of the fierce bloodsheds and persecutions which met the early Christians in other countries. The Irish, already religious in their own way, and with a spirit of intelligent inquiry indicative of their advanced civilisation, shrewdly inquired of their Christian teachers, if there was no salvation for man without the knowledge of the Gospels of Christ, what then was to become of the souls of their fathers, who had lived moral and virtuous lives assisting the necessitous, righting the oppressed, and punishing the wicked. Were they to suffer in hell to eternity for not believing and obeying doctrines of which they had never heard or could have known while on earth?

This was a question not easily answered, and they were therefore permitted to believe that the spirits of their fathers were allowed to wander on earth about their old abodes, and in the sunny places they had loved on earth, there to remain until the great day of general judgment, when it was to be hoped that if their conduct till then was approved of, the Son of Man, in his mercy, would admit them into heaven; and these spirits becoming at times visible and visiting mortals occasionally in peace and kindliness are the Irish fairies, the "Doonia Sighe," or men of peace.

These fairies are always supposed to live principally in raths or forts, and this is another proof of the truth of the foregoing hypothesis. The forts or raths are by most modern writers considered to have been the work of the Danes while in Ireland. Now it is well known that during the sojourn of the Danes in that country they dwelt only along the coast, and in maritime towns, whereas all these forts are in the interior of the country.

The traditions of the people, therefore, come nearer the true origin. They tell us, that in the early ages when druidism prevailed, these forts were the dwelling places of the natives. The country then was full of jungles, brushwood, and noxious animals; they, therefore, erected their dwellings on hills and high grounds, and in order to facilitate communication by signals of fire for mutual assistance in cases of emergency, from every fort in Ireland another can be seen. The fort was not the dwelling of one man or one family, but of a whole tribe or clan. Within the circle of the fort were erected houses, or more properly speaking, booths, of hurdles and wickerwork; and these were so contrived by moveable partitions that the dwelling could be enlarged or contracted as occasion required.

It was also an age of predatory warfare. The strong oppressed the weak, and the circular ditch and mound was the best defence they could devise. The more powerful chiefs had two and sometimes three ditches around their dwellings. In cases of attack, they manned the outer fosse, and when forced from that they had a second or third to fall back on.

Druidism being the religion of the land, and because they prayed facing the sun, supposed to be the dwelling place of Baal, every fort has not only an opening on the east, but the enclosed plane also inclines in that direction that they might the more readily perceive the rising of their god.

These forts, then, having been the homes of the ancient Irish, whom St. Patrick tacitly allowed to wander about their old dwellings, are the chief residences of the fairies of the present day, and are still held in such veneration that the plough never passes over them, nor will an Irish peasant even break a branch from the hoary hawthorn which has grown there whole ages unmolested.

The great night of the festival of Samhin seems to be peculiarly honoured by the fairies, and the mountain peasantry believing them to possess a kind of semi-mortality, they still hospitably preserve a part of the hallowe'en supper, which is left in a convenient place for their especial use. They are supposed to be very desirous of stealing young children, brides and beautiful girls, hence the tale, as I have given it, was firmly believed in that neighbourhood and perhaps is still. A male fairy is a *dunne sighe*, and a female a *bean sigh* pronounced *banshee*; and are supposed to attach themselves to certain old Milesian families, and to foretell their deaths by singing a beautiful dirge about the house for some nights previous.

And now, Mr. Pickwick, I cannot quote written authorities for the foregoing more than Hesiod or Herodotus could for theirs, namely, that it is the tradition of the natives. I have had it from an old man, who never spoke a word of the English language, but who could recite more of the genuine poetry of Ossian than M'Pherson, Blair, and Johnson could produce altogether.

Page 53 (7) When a person has been drowned in a lake, and the body cannot be found, a sheaf of corn is prepared and sent adrift on the water, when it will float about and finally become stationary over the corpse.

Page 67 (8) In a wild tract of the county of Donegal lies the celebrated lake of Lough Derg, about the middle of the lake is a small island, which contains St. Patrick's purgatory, much frequented by penitent pilgrims. It is a dark cavern of some extent where the penitent, after having fasted and prayed for some days in a little chapel, is obliged to watch and pray for one night or more, and with the mind and body weakened by the previous preparations, the awful noises caused by the echoing of the dashing waves among the caverned rocks, the dim twinkling light of a few tapers, and the predisposition of the penitent's mind, a night spent in that cave watching in fear and trembling is a most trying ordeal.

Page 85 A line giving the greatest length of Ireland would extend from Fairforeland, in the county of Antrim to the old head of Kinsale. Another from the hill of Howth to Blacksod Bay, near Galway, would describe its greatest breadth, and these lines would intersect at Moat Farrel, in the county of Longford. A circle of six miles radius round that point would embrace the birth-place of the celebrated Malone, of the Irish Handel Carolan, of Oliver Goldsmith, of the Count O'Reilly named in Don Juan, of Maria Edgworth, of her uncle, the Abbe Edgworth, who attended Lewis XVII. on the scaffold, and of the humble, artless, and supremely beautiful, but unfortunate Mary Flinn, the heroine of the poem of Frantic Mary.

About forty-five years ago, when I was quite a lad, I passed some weeks in that part of the country, and heard almost every one talk of the beautiful Mary Flinn, I therefore went the following Sunday afternoon to see her at the dance at Phil M'Glinn's, at Coolaherty. It was a beautiful little valley, through which ran a clear limped stream. Before we could see "the dance" we could hear the clear tones of poor "Blind Charley's" fiddle rising on the gentle breezes among the echoing hills.

Never have I seen anything since or before that seemed so delightful, or that filled my mind with such happy impressions, every one was so becomingly dressed, so cheerful, so decorous; so modest, and so happy; but conspicuous among them all, for simple elegance, modesty, and surpassing loveliness, was the beautiful Mary Flinn. She wore a crimson stuff dress, tightly fitting about the throat, a green silk necktie, her hair neatly curled in front, secured behind by a comb and no other head-dress; she danced with the lightness of a fairy. I remember yet every plait and fold of her dress, every look, word, and motion, even to the tie of her shoes; a wreath of hair escaped from her comb in the dancing, and perhaps added to her gracefulness. But alas! for the instability of all sublunary happiness; just as all were intently absorbed in the delightful contemplation of the scene, as the "Double Petticoatee" was being executed by eight couples with graceful agility, and even before "the plate was sent round" for poor Blind Charley, Old Father John was seen coming cantering down the mountain road on his well known grey mare; away flew every soul at the dance helter-skelter, and many a young woman who tumbled in the scamper, was glad to accept the assistance of a half-rejected lover, while two stalwart fellows ran away with "Blind Charley" and concealed him in an adjoining copse-wood.

Even then I was a dabbler in poetry. In the course of the ensuing week, I wrote a song in praise of "Charming Mary Flinn," which after some time became very popular. I wen with others more than once to her mother's cottage, and joine the circle of youngsters among the spinning wheels, around the hearth, and often sung my song of "Charming Mary Flinn" to her while "seated on the end of her stool."

Some time afterwards she was seduced by a half-pay officer, a Captain Gray, to whom she was betrayed by her own aunt, who lived in his service, but who like herself, expected he would have married her—she afterwards attempted suicide as described in the text; on her recovery she disappeared, and none knew what had become of her, Captain Grey drank himself into insanity and ended his days in a Lunatic Asylum. Her mother died of a broken heart. Many a time on winter nights when the youngsters met together has that song been sung in tears to the memory of poor Mary Flinn.

In my subsequent rambles, I remained some time in Liverpool. There was in those days a public house in Hood street, called the Playhouse Tavern. It was the principal rendezvous of the middle class of prostitutes, such as expected to pick up their victims among the playgoing gents, and they generally whiled away the time there till the play was over.

They kept good whiskey in the Playhouse Tavern, and it was consequently much frequented by Irishmen. I went there one night along with some of my companions, we made ourselves very comfortable with whiskey punch, jokes, anecdotes, and songs. In staring about I saw a bevy of unfortunate girls in an inner room, the door having been left ajar, and among them with faded silk dress, rings, chains, and a high-crowned hat, after the manner of the Welsh girls, I saw and knew at the first glance the poor, unhappy, long lost Mary Flinn. But oh! how changed; her cheeks were now somewhat hollow. the pure roses gone, and in their stead a deep crimson, broken and curdled, and the eyes that once shone so deep and gentle, were now dim, dull, and restless. The whole expression of her countenance was sadly changed. Never did I see the ravages of vice and sorrow so strikingly displayed. I watched her for some time in deep commiseration, thinking of the time when she was the pride of a whole country side—so lovely, so cheerful, so innocent.

I was called on for a song in my turn, and at once commenced "Charming Mary Flinn." Before I got half through the first verse, she started, listened, became deadly pale, and put her handkerchief to her face. She sat still to the conclusion of the song, but I could plainly see, like rising waves, the swelling suppressed sobs working up her throat, and her whole frame quivering.

When I had concluded, she arose and did not appear again until we left. When outside I saw her again, she stole up to me quite timidly, and putting a slip of paper into my hand hurried out of sight; it contained her address, with a request that I would call to see her next day, at four o'clock in the afternoon, being Sunday.

I did call, and never shall I forget that interview. She told me her whole story up to the present hour. It was, in fact, a history of her feelings, her sorrows, and her sufferings. She wept until I began to fear for her reason. I felt assured that the very vestal virgins in their sanctuaries did not detest her mode of life more than she did. She had tried every plan to avoid it, but found herself outlawed everywhere. She could obtain no service nor countenance from any one; and yet it was evident that her woman's soul cherished deeply that timid shrinking from impurity, which, unless under the influence of inebriation, never wholly abandons the female heart.

I have had great pleasure since in reflecting that I obtained for her the protection of a lady, where she led a most exemplary life for some years, and was subsequently married to a worthy bricklayer in Birkenhead, where she may be living yet for all I know.

ERRATA.

Page 25—for "1864," read 1846.
Page 36, Line 1st—for "genily," read gently.
Page 39, Line 2nd—for "pears," read pease.
Page 101, fourth line of 2nd verse—read "Delightful though beguiling."

SUBSCRIBERS' NAMES.

Being no Ulster King at Arms, I have followed the Order of my Canvass.

	Copies.
Rt. Hon. Lord Farnham	10
Isaac Holden, Esq, Archt.	10
Major Porteus	10
I. M. Bennett, Mayor	10
Isaac Holden, Jun., Archt.	5
John Holden, Architect	5
Wm. Fairbairn, Esq., LL.D.	10
Thomas Fairbairn, Esq.	10
Mr. Henry Ledger, Builder	5
Mr. Wm. Higgins, Builder	5
Mr. Alderman J. Goadsby	10
Mr. Alderman A. Heywood	10
Jas. P. Holden, Esq., Archt.	4
Mr. Henry Adshead	5
Mr. Joseph Woodward	2
Mr. Jas. Conuell, Cloone	4
Mr. S. Robinson, Newtonheath	2
Mr. Thos. Tully, Builder	2
Mr. Mark Cooper, Rumford Street	1
Mr. T. Moran, Plasterer	3
Mr. W. Moran, Plasterer	1
Mr. E. M Carthy, Salesman	3
Mr. P. M'Carthy, Livesey Street	2
Mr. J. Dixon, Druggist	4
Mr. M. Daly, Clerk	2
Mr. B. Kiernan	1
Mr. P. Green, Plasterer	2
Mr. J. Sellars, Portland St.	4
Mr. M. Nelus, George Leigh Street	1
Mr. J. M'Connell, Westhoughton	2
Mr. W. S. Hall, City Road	1
P. Mollay, M.D.	2
Jos. Heron, T. C.	3
Mr. J. Nixon, Eccles	1
Mr. H. Brierley, Chapman Street	1
Mr. M. Connell, Carniu.	2
R. O'Reilly, Esq., B. J. Duff	3
Mr. J. O'Neil, Oldham Road	3
Mr. P. Connell, Springtown	2
Mr. Thos. Flood, Drumrora.	1
Mr. J. C. Sellars, Birkenhead	2
Mr. Jas. Connell, Mason	1
Mr. J. Melanny, Boyle	1
A. O'Reilly, Esq., Beltrasna	5
Mr. P. M'Lauren, Plasterer	1
Mr. Miles Shields, Buxton St.	1

INDEX.

	Page
Preface	3
The Albert Memorial	7
The Prestwich Asylum	17
The Firehorse	25
Winter in Manchester	29
Epithalamium	33
Cotter's Sunday Morning	35
Dunbinni's Bride	45
The Gregory Day	57
Little Dora	62
Lines on 1848	70
Frantic Mary	74
The Sheebeen House	86
My Once Happy Home	92
On Lord Palmerston's Birthday	95
A Dream of Youth	99
My Summer Days are over	101
The Home I left Behind	103
Tir na Hoigdha	105
Elleen a Roon	106
The Coolin	107
Notes	10

www.ingramcontent.com/pod-product-compliance
Lightning Source LLC
Chambersburg PA
CBHW030905170426
43193CB00009BA/734